Easter

The Great Mary

A journey to discover Mary Magdalene

Michael Bever

© Copyright 2021 Michael Bever

All rights reserved.
No part of this publication may be reproduced, stored in a retrieval system, or transmitted, in any form or by any means, electronic, mechanical, photocopying, recording or otherwise, without the prior written permission of the publisher.

British Library Cataloguing in Publication Data.
A catalogue record for this book is available from the British Library

978 0 86071 853 6

A Commissioned Publication Printed by
MOORLEYS
Print, Design & Publishing
info@moorleys.co.uk • www.moorleys.co.uk

Mary Magdalene: who was she?

Michael Bever invites you to come on a journey to discover Mary Magdalene

Robert Runcie, whenever he wanted to have a private conversation with one of his students at Cuddesdon, would offer the invitation, 'Come, walk with me'. I invite you to come walk with me on a journey to discover Mary Magdalene. There is no set map for our journey to follow. Our journey will be like a treasure hunt where we move from clue to clue. Hopefully, if we follow the clues successfully, we shall reach our destination.

My journey began in the middle of Lent 2018. I found myself in the garden trying to rescue some fiendishly barbed blackberries whose supports had collapsed the previous autumn in the high winds. I was quietly working away but needed something to think about. I had been fascinated by the enigma of Mary Magdalene for a while and she came very forcibly into my mind. I had to work on this.

Our journey begins fairly straightforwardly. There are things that we traditionally think we know about her from the mundane to the unsubstantiated flights of fancy and legend. We need to start from the simplest first principles.

Her name is Mary, which is unfortunately the commonest of Hebrew female names and so could lead to confusion.

Traditionally, we understand her name as meaning 'Mary who came from Magdala'. Professor Joan Taylor in her paper (*Palestine Exploration Quarterly 146.3* 2014) has shown that, although there were many places throughout the Holy Land with composite names, the second half of which is *migdal* (tower), none can fit the bill for a Magdala for Mary. There is no place that can be firmly identified as Magdala in the right area at the right time.

When the Gospels describe people as 'coming from' somewhere they usually do it differently from how Mary is described. Joseph of Arimathea is, in Greek, Joseph from Arimathea; likewise Jesus in John 1:45 is son of Joseph from Nazareth; Simon of Cyrene is the Cyrenian (a straightforward adjective). Mary's description is not a straightforward adjective though it 'could' mean the 'Magdala Mary'. Is there a better way to understand her name?

Professor Taylor 'suggests' that 'the Magdalene' could be a nickname given to Mary in the way that Jesus gave nicknames to other disciples. In which case she is 'the Tower' in the same way that Peter is 'the Rock', and the sons of Zebedee are Boanerges 'sons of thunder', the noisy ones. Prof. Taylor suggests that many other names of disciples can be treated in the same way. While I do not think this is the best explanation, I do find her conclusion on this interesting and helpful. "Mary is in a special category of 'called' people…………and that the epithet is indicative of who she was……"

Professor C.K.Barrett in his commentary on John *(The Gospel according to John* 1958*)* points out that Mary Magdalene is a Crucifixion and Resurrection character. This applies to every incident in which she is mentioned except Luke 8:2 which I suggest is his variant of Mark 15:40-41. I regard this as a 'rogue', if not malicious, verse on which I will comment later. If Magdalene is a crucifixion, resurrection name then I do not think Jesus is in a position to be giving out nicknames from the cross! If he gave it earlier why are we not told? I suggest it is more likely to be a title that Mary had in the earliest church, at least by the time the earliest oral account of the Passion was circulating. We need to look for a meaning of the Hebrew behind Magdalene. We have already heard about the 'tower' (or 'the woman in the tower'). We can now add 'the exalted one'. Hebrew has such a fluidity of meaning in its words that must (for the experts) be both exciting and frustrating. Here, we have 'the epithets indicative of who she was', 'the Tower' and 'the Exalted One'.

My thinking now led me to take down from my bookshelf Professor C.F.D.Moule's *Idiom Book of New Testament Greek* 1953. Here I was reminded that the definite article can be used as the relative pronoun. Does this help to explain the expression "Mary the Magdalene"? Should we be hearing more clearly 'Mary who is Magdalene'. Mary who is 'the exalted one', Mary who is 'the tower'.

Thus far we have been able to travel in a fairly straight line. From now on we move on what Gunther Grass would have called a 'crab walk'. By moving sideways we move, like the crab, forwards. Movements seem to build up in significance. We will now need to keep in mind all possible indicators of Mary Magdalene from the Canonical Gospels and Epistles, to all the other literature of the early church, to Jewish references, to the writings that Irenaeus, called by Bart D. Ehrman 'the enforcer', managed to expunge from the tradition but might represent the tradition of other Christian groups, to later Christian writings. We only have a small fraction of early 'Christian' literature remaining to us. A comment here may shed a little light on something elsewhere. This will all give us a richer picture of whom she was.

Let us go back to Luke 8:2.

To put this verse into context we need to consider the character of the emergent church. Sadly, hard and fast evidence for the period 33-80AD is very sparse. Once again it is hints here and there. We usually turn in the first instant to Acts, Paul's Epistles, Hebrews, 1 Peter and the Didache[1]. The church, not yet Christianity, begins as a sub-sect of Judaism. No doubt here there were many different emphases as there always are with new movements, some more radical, others more conservative. To begin with it would appear to cohere around the prominent disciples in Jerusalem. How many of the original disciples continue to remain active in the mission and how, we do not know. Initially the Temple would have been the focal point of the group but that is replaced by the hope for a 'new' Temple following Jesus' teaching

---

[1] Its full title is 'The Teaching of the Lord, by the Twelve Disciples, to the Gentiles' and sees itself as a statement of the essentials of the Jesus movement as understood by his early followers. Much of it is taken up with teaching on Jesus' summary of the Law - what it means to love God and love your neighbour as yourself. It is now thought to come from the Apostolic period.

and a longing for the First Temple to be restored. This longing is shown in Hebrews and Revelation. On to this scene from almost out of nowhere comes Paul.

He has a bad reputation as a persecutor of the Jerusalem Church. He says he has been for 3 years in 'Arabia' and then starts his 14 years evangelism in Syria and Cilicia. We have no direct evidence for what he achieves in that period.

Our primary evidence for his activity is his epistles beginning with 1 Thessalonians but, most importantly, with Galatians. Reconciling his epistles with Acts has been a major scholarly endeavour for many years. Maybe we should just accept that they are irreconcilable and follow Paul in the first instant. However, we may be cautious about his absolute objectivity. Objectivity is difficult for any of us when presenting our viewpoint. Paul could be biased in his own favour.

Paul is known as the 'apostle of salvation without the Law'. If the Jerusalem Church is true to its loyalty to the First Temple and its rejection of the Mosaic Law we would expect it to be as antinomian as Paul. Salvation for the Jerusalem church also goes back to Abraham and not to the Deuteronomists' Moses and the Law. The Didache shows that there is a law and it is Jesus' two laws, which it then goes on to elucidate. Guidance needs to be given or how else do we know how to behave. Paul himself gives guidance. In Revelation there is a great Assize. People need to know how they are going to be judged. No doubt it is all about degree. It is very easy to appear to be too lax.

Divisions in the Church -of which there are plenty in the early years - often seem to be due to personalities and rivalry over how they and others see their significance. We shall see more evidence of this later. This is undoubtedly true with Paul.

Where is the major problem for the Jerusalem/Hebrew Church with Paul. I do not think it is over circumcision. Paul says it isn't. Often division comes with loyalty to social customs. These define the character of a group. What is trivial to one is important to another. I suggest the real problem is over dietary requirements and the situations that lead others to questions your loyalty to the group. If there are problems with dietary conformity there can be no table fellowship, and therefore no sharing in the Eucharist. This is the subject of the big row in Antioch between Paul and Peter who is conservative on the matter. Because of his 'vision' on this matter Peter moves across to a Pauline position. The vision, if it happened, only makes sense if it happens after the confrontation with Paul and not where Acts wants to place it.

The problem with this digression here is that it opens up a huge field of study that cannot be handled in this short paper.

When we turn again to Acts we see that it would appear to offer an idealistic picture of the Church, probably, as it was at the time of writing c80AD. The earlier problems in the Church are no longer active. All is well.

In Acts we have a book of two halves. The first is centred on Peter, the second on Paul. Together they make a unity. Whether Peter and Paul are fellow workers in Rome we are not told. Rome is the climax of the Lukan story. The writer seems to be ignorant of the Pauline epistles and so does not include anything about Paul's desire to go further West in the Empire, or he discounts it. His story is that all is now well for his church. 'And he lived there two whole years….preaching…and teaching about the Lord Jesus Christ quite openly and unhindered' (Acts 28:30-31). The speculated on next volume is unnecessary and, probably, never existed.

Luke/Acts is the written account of the Pauline faction. The Hebrew Church is most significantly represented in the works of John. An early example of the rancorous division in Asia Minor may be seen in the Letters to the Seven Churches in Revelation. Here is a battle ground spread across Asia Minor to Ephesus. Dr Barker (cf. M.Barker *The Revelation of Jesus Christ* 2000) identifies Paul as Balaam and Lydia as Jezebel (Rev. 2:12-29). I find her arguments 'persuasive' though they may be regarded as 'speculative'. The issue at Pergamum is food sacrificed to idols and fornication. Fornication is probably just general laxness. At Thyatira the charge is the same. Here Lydia probably belongs to the trade guild where there are all sorts of dangers for the Church, especially in their dinners. In the letter to the Ephesians (Rev 2:1-7) the Nicolaitans are also mentioned as in the letter to Pergamum. They are immoral and eat food sacrificed to idols. Here, clearly, the problem is food and its acceptability. It could be that all these letters are veiled attacks on churches founded by Paul, perhaps in his missionary work in Cilicia and Antioch at the beginning of his labours, especially if John's letters in Revelation are early.

According to Paul (Romans 14: 1 Cor. 8 and 10) his approach to food laws is very nuanced and is integrally connected with each of the great commandments of love of God and love of neighbour. It is never a matter of a free for all, anything goes. No doubt his approach lays him open to accusations of betrayal from his opponents and to an over-relaxed approach by some individuals and some in his congregations.

By placing Luke 8:2 earlier in his gospel than Mark does, Luke is able to begin his denigration of Mary Magdalene. She is one from whom evil spirits had been cast out. There is no mention of these in Mark. Mary, for Luke, is just a weak character whom Jesus has rescued and who has become a devoted follower. In this one verse, in these few words, Luke introduces the idea that Mary Magdalene has a psychiatric problem. Mental problems are prone to recur. She will always be unreliable.

We now come to the Crucifixion and the Resurrection stories. At the Crucifixion Mary Magdalene is always named first among the little group of women (except in John). Does this signify a leadership role? In the Resurrection stories in the Synoptic Gospels Mary Magdalene is again named first in a group of women. But it is the group who go to the tomb. It is the group in Matthew who take hold of Jesus feet when they meet him in the way. They are given a message for the disciples but we are never told if they deliver it. In Luke when the women led by Mary Magdalene report their experience to the disciples we are told "these words seemed to them an idle tale, and they did not believe them". Mary Magdalene and her female companions are unreliable witnesses. In Luke 24:12, which has a good textual pedigree but is usually put as a foot note, Peter "rose and went to the tomb; stooping and looking in, he saw the linen clothes by themselves; and he went home wondering at what had happened". This is similar to John's account and we wonder if they knew a similar tradition. If Peter did later go and tell the others then I am sure he would have been believed. In all the resurrection appearances Peter is significant.

When we come to John's Gospel the situation has changed completely. Mary Magdalene is now on an individual personal quest of significance. Here in John 20 we have three stories that sit awkwardly in sequence but can be read more easily side by side. First, a grieving women comes to be at the grave. There is no task to be done.

The anointing has already been correctly carried out. The stone is removed and she fears grave robbers. She goes and tells Simon Peter. Simon Peter and the other disciple make their discovery and go home. Only the other disciple has any realisation of what has happened. 'For as yet they do not know the scripture'. Then Mary Magdalene has her encounter with Jesus. She only recognises him when he addresses her by name. It is his living words that convince her. Here she alone holds him or rather goes on holding him. She is told to stop what she is doing. She is then given the great double message of Resurrection and Ascension. She then goes and tells the disciples. She says to them what he said to her. It is interesting (vid. Barrett op.cit. p.467) that the word 'Magdalene' is omitted in verses 1 and 18 in *sin*.[2] Did the Syrian Church think of a different Mary as going to the tomb?

Before we move on we need to reflect further on Mary Magdalene's significance in John 20. Mary Magdalene's encounter with Jesus is one of a number of incidents that are unique to John's Gospel. This does not mean that they were not known elsewhere in the tradition that is now lost to us, but it does suggest that these episodes had special significance for John. This is true for the encounter of Mary with the 'risen' Christ on Easter morning.

How are we to regard this encounter? We need to note that it has something of the vision about it. It stands somewhere on the borderland between the Jesus of history and the Christ of faith. I suggest we need to stand also in that strange position. If we just accept the story as straightforward history we are in danger of missing its greater significance in John's Gospel. If we deny its historicity, as some would, and see it as a theological/literary device upon which John hangs his Christology, we put ourselves in the place of never knowing what to follow as tentative fact anywhere. This is particularly true in this chapter where Mary is not

---

[2] *sin* is the textual symbol for the Sinaitic Syriac [Old Syriac] Version.

the only character, as we shall see, who could be dismissed as a theological/literary device. Since the community for which this gospel was written was probably very familiar with Mary Magdalene and the tradition attached to her, how would you pull off this trick of establishing an historical falsehood as historical fact. I humbly suggest it would not survive long.

Mary Magdalene has a fundamental part to play in John 20, the culmination of the first edition of the work. We too easily see the Resurrection as the climax of the gospel story, but it isn't. That is not reached until the final word of chapter 20. For our writer, Mary is one of the carriers to its completion of his Christology. Many have recognised that for John, uniquely, the Crucifixion and the Resurrection are two halves of one event, the exaltation and glorification of Jesus. This is the exaltation and glorification for which Jesus has prayed: 'So now Father, glorify me in your own presence with the glory that I had in your presence before the world existed' (John 17:5). On the cross he is 'lifted up', 'raised' and 'glorified'. His resurrection begins on the cross.

In its essence resurrection is not a post mortem event. This was recognised in the early church (e.g. in the Gospel of Philip, which says: 'Those who say that the Lord died first and rose up are in error, for he rose up first and died. If one does not first attain the resurrection, will he not die? As God lives he would be [dead]'.[3] Jesus was first raised at his Baptism. While his exaltation has been achieved at the Crucifixion/Resurrection it remains to be 'actualised' by the Ascension. Mary Magdalene is the messenger of that actualisation. Is she also the person who 'sees' it when Jesus says to her, 'I am ascending to my Father and your Father, to my God and your God'? Is Mary Magdalene responsible for the doctrine of the Ascension?

What we are given in the whole of John 20, is the climactic conclusion of John's story. It is a confirmatory book end to John 1, and, as I have said, to Jesus prayer in chapter 17. Jesus is 'from the beginning', that is, from 'Day One', the heavenly realm where God is. He has come from there and John 20 tells us he is going back there (or has gone back there). He came to his own and, as the gospel story tells us, most did not recognise

---

[3] The Gospel of Philip is now recognised as preserving material from the early Church.

him. To those who did recognise him- who he was and what he did- he gave the power to become children of God. Mary Magdalene was pre-eminently one such person. So also was Thomas. Do we want to make him a theological/literary device existing solely to deliver the Christological statement, 'My Lord and my God'? To Thomas is given the great cry of recognition from John 1. But the story does not end there with one man's recognition. Recognition is there also for all who have not seen in the flesh but believe i.e. all those in John's young Church. You can believe because you can have confidence in John's message. This is declared strongly in the last verse of the chapter. It is stated even more strongly in the addendum of John 21 where John, or his updater, declares his testimony to be true.

John's final Ascension chapter is again the Synoptic/Acts story compressed, like so much in the gospel. There is a Great Commission akin to Matthew's and the 'Spirit' is poured out, Pentecost. The Spirit is the power for their mission. They can be the instruments of others' recognition.

All this is the result of the 'completion' that Mary Magdalene is entrusted to announce.

When Paul quotes the witnesses of the Resurrection in 1 Corinthians 15 he does not mention Mary Magdalene who is the most prominent witness in the Gospels especially in John. Nor does he seem to show any knowledge of the Easter story as told in the Four Gospels. Does he not know it, or does he just choose to ignore it and base his understanding of Jesus resurrection elsewhere? We can only guess what he had against Mary Magdalene. Was she a very prominent member of the Hebrew Church with which he was struggling? Is this the first example of someone being airbrushed out of the Christian story? Is Paul's opposition to Mary Magdalene what lies behind 1 Corinthians 11? Luke is writing the history of the Church from the Petrine/Pauline perspective. When it comes to the Passion, though, he is constrained to use the already widely known narrative. However, after Easter when the two disciples return to Jerusalem from Emmaus they are told, "The Lord has risen indeed, and he has appeared to Simon". This seems to indicate that the Lord has appeared to Simon, though we are not told how. This 'supports' Paul (1 Corinthians 15:5) 'that he appeared to Cephas, then the twelve'.

Before we leave the Mary Magdalene of the canonical records we need to go back to the Easter story one more time. What might have been the nature and the significance of her experience at the empty tomb and her encounter with the risen Jesus?

What is the significance of the tomb? That it was significant is shown by the Emperor Constantine building a complex around the site of Calvary and the tomb of Jesus. This complex is to be the new Temple. Is it a commonplace by Constantine's time that the tomb represents the Holy of Holies?

Mary looks in and sees two angels in white at either end of the grave slab. Blood may have leaked from the body onto the slab. There would have been the strong smell of the spices. 75lbs of myrrh and aloes is an excessive amount (c.f. the excessive amount of wine at the wedding at Cana). That amount of myrrh might have been intended for embalming but that was a lengthy process for which there was not enough time. Myrrh was also the dominant temple perfume used for anointing. John is perhaps suggesting that this is a superabundance of the anointing oil for anointing the High Priest. What Mary is looking into is the Holy of Holies after the Atonement blood has been offered by the High Priest. Jesus is both Priest and Offering. Linen was the material of the High Priestly robe for the Atonement. Here now it is not the usual one piece garment but a series of strips (*othonia* pieces of fine linen). The spices would have been spread between the strips (vid Barrett op.cit.supra pp.465;365). These strips remind me of the linen strips in which Jesus was swaddled at his birth (Luke 2:12). Barker (*Christmas. The Original Story,* 2008 pp.75-76) suggests his clothes are mentioned because the clothing of the 'newly born' High Priest was an important part of his becoming the Son. Here the divine is clothed in the human. The Glory is made incarnate. This is the glory to which Jesus prayed to return (John 17:5). Might the pile of discarded fine linen grave clothes signify the reversal of the process? The incarnate has been glorified. The High Priest has returned whence he came. He is no longer here. Matthew tells us there has been a thunder clap and the sealed stone is rolled away. If John knew there had been thunder when the stone was rolled away does he echo here with the rolling away of the stone the separating of the veil at Jesus death in Matthew, Mark and Luke and his appearance as Son of God, the Righteous Man? Does the rolled away stone represent that same veil of the Temple through which the High Priest emerges when he has completed the atonement sacrifice? In the Holy of Holies there was the Mercy Seat, in Greek *hilasterion,* in Hebrew *kapporeth.* It was a slab of gold with an angel figure at either end. On the Day of Atonement the High Priest sprinkled blood on the front of the Mercy Seat. This becomes an early, important interpretation of the death and resurrection of Jesus c.f. Romans 3:25 and Hebrews 9:11-14. This is Mary's first vision. Is she the originator of this interpretation? Does this vision perhaps give us the origin of all the other 'empty tomb' accounts?

The second is her encounter with Jesus. This is perhaps the prototype of her other encounters with Jesus after the resurrection that are given in the non-canonical accounts. Maybe there were others in the oral tradition.

First she is seen weeping by the angels. 'Why are you weeping?' they ask. The Old Syriac adds 'for whom are you looking?' This addition may be a scribal error from v15, or it may reflect Matthew, or it could be original. I suggest it is implied in the question. Weeping is a normal human reaction to loss. In the East, great wailing is an important part of all funerals. I suggest, though, that there is more going on here than a matter of human loss. Jesus then asks Mary the same question. There is the implication that her response of weeping is inappropriate. You are doing the wrong thing. Matthew spells this out clearly. 'He is not here for he has been raised'. According to Isaiah 25:8, in the new age, after swallowing up death for ever, God 'will wipe away tears from all faces'.

This is what Mary should be recognising and apparently is not. This is the new age, humanity has been restored. Here is 'resurrection'.

She turns round but does not recognise Jesus. She thinks he is the gardener. This seems a natural reaction, but did places like this have gardeners? Is there here another theological subtlety? Would John's readers have recognised here Adam the original gardener from whom humanity's separation from the tree of life had flowed. Are we being pointed to the 'second Adam' who restores humanity's access to the tree of life. This is a powerful Christian image but one that does not occur in Jesus' own teaching. He then calls her by her name, and she recognises him.

I am intrigued by Mary Magdalene's address to Jesus as *Rabbouni*. The NEB translates the word from the Aramaic as 'My Teacher' not from John's Greek translation as 'Teacher'. I suspect there is something hidden here. Elsewhere in the Gospels Jesus is simply addressed as Rabbi. Mary's title must be special and say something about their relationship. I am reminded of Peter's request to Mary in the Gospel of Mary[4] to reveal to them the teaching that Jesus gave to her but not to them. Mary replies, 'What is hidden from you I will proclaim to you'. Mary seems to be known as someone who received special teaching. This is interesting as the term Rabbi is not one that is used in the canonical early church. The term for Jesus there becomes 'Lord'. As we have seen above Mary is given the message for the disciples of the glorification of Jesus, his return to the Father to be the Son. She announces this to them with the words, 'I have seen the Lord'. I have seen the Son, Yahweh, Adonai, the Lord. Is she the originator of the term 'Lord' that later Thomas echoes? I have just questions; no firm answers.

We are left wondering what other subtleties might be lurking beneath the surface that John's readers would have been aware of and we are not.

Before we leave this we need just to pause and see what the Peter and the beloved disciple incident at the tomb might be saying to us.

We are told that Peter 'followed' the other disciple. 'Followed' is a significant word in John's vocabulary. It may be intended here to subordinate Peter to the beloved disciple. While the other disciple does not immediately go into the tomb, perhaps because of his priestly office, when he does go in, we are told, 'he sees and believes'. Exactly what he saw we are not told. Maybe he has a similar experience to Mary. Peter has no such experience. The beloved disciple has priority of faith.

John 21, the later addition to the original book, would appear to be about the association and contrast of Peter and the beloved disciple. Is rivalry between Peter and the beloved disciple expressed in verses 20-23, where the beloved disciple is already doing what Peter has just been bidden to

---

[4] The Gospel of Mary, part of the Berlin Gnostic Codex known since 1896, is believed to originate in 2nd century. It has been suggested it could be early 1st century.

do i.e. follow? Once more his superiority to Peter is implied. This could be a personal rivalry or one between the Churches represented by the beloved disciple and Peter. Either the beloved disciple holds himself superior to Peter or that is the belief of the Church that he represents. Here is one more indicator of the 'differences' that existed in the earliest Church.

Mary Magdalene now disappears from the canonical records. It may be appropriate to note at this point that visionary experiences in the Christian story are not as odd as we might naturally think in our 21st century. They are everywhere, and they permeate both the Old and New Testaments. It is perhaps difficult to separate what is physical from what is visionary in the resurrection story. Mary Magdalene does not recognise a physical Jesus, but does recognise his voice. Paul who has no claim to any physical contact with Jesus, can still forcefully claim he has received a resurrection appearance (Gal 1:12). This must be through the voice speaking to him on the Damascus Road. We should keep this in mind when we turn to other sources for Mary Magdalene. Visions are an accepted part of life.

If the early Church in Jerusalem gave Mary Magdalene the epithet 'exalted' she must have been very significant. We can speculate that this status may not have made her popular with everyone. Even if Mary was not herself numbered among the Pillars of the Church (Gal 2:9) she would have been very close to them. This would have made her unpopular with those who did not like being ruled from Jerusalem. There must have been daily out-workings of her significance.

I would like now to turn to the extra-canonical books that refer to Mary Magdalene, especially the Gospel of Mary. These cannot be dismissed out of hand with the broad swipe of being 'Gnostic' as they do reflect what was believed by certain branches of the very early church. The Gospel of Mary is a very old document that is generally accepted as being about Mary Magdalene. Sadly, it is an incomplete text with great gaps. Karen L. King *(The Gospel of Mary Magdalene, 1994)* believes the setting in the first section of the text is a post-resurrection appearance of the Saviour in which the Saviour is in dialogue with the disciples. He leaves them distraught and anxious. Mary speaks up with words of comfort and encouragement. Peter asks Mary to share with them any special teaching she received from the Saviour. Peter said to Mary. "Sister, we know that the Saviour loved you more than the rest of the women. Tell us the words of the Saviour which you remember - which you know but we do not, nor have we heard them". Mary recounts a conversation she had with the Saviour about visions. Mary said, "I saw the Lord in a vision and I said to him, 'Lord I saw you today in a vision'". Her vision does not meet with universal approval. We are told Peter also opposed her in regard to these matters. "Did he then speak secretly with a woman, in preference to us, and not openly? Are we to turn back and all listen to her? Did he prefer her to us?" Peter is opposed to her position. Karen L. King concludes that the Gospel of Mary is about inter-Christian controversies, the reliability of the disciples' witness, the validity of teachings given to the disciples through post-resurrection revelation and vision, and the leadership of women. Peter has the same opposing role to Mary, because she is a woman, in the Gospel of Thomas[5] and in Pistis Sophia[6]. In the final scene of the Gospel of Mary, Levi, in defence of Mary and her teaching, tells Peter, "Surely the Saviour knows her very well. That is why he loved her more than us." King also says that the gospel exposes the erroneous view that Mary Magdalene is a prostitute for what it is - a piece of theological fiction or slander.

The high point for Luke's Acts is when Peter jumps ship, deserts Jerusalem and joins Paul after his vision, his own Damascus Road experience. Our canon of scripture blurs over this fundamental division and makes us think we are all one. The Gospel of Mary disabuses us of this naivety. Perhaps the continuing division between East and West should tell us still that we are not one.

We need to decide which Mary is the subject of the Gospel of Mary. The weight of opinion would seem to be in favour of Mary Magdalene. However, Stephen J. Shoemaker argues in favour of Mary, the mother of Jesus. This would comply with Jesus loving her more than the other disciples, being his greatest disciple and also for her being the central figure of Christianity. He draws attention to the fact that when Jesus says to her, "Blessed are you, that you did not waver at the sight of me" it is similar to when Elizabeth says to the Virgin Mary, "Blessed are you

---

[5] The Gospel of Thomas discovered at Nag Hammadi in 1946. Dated AD60 to AD140. Mainly sayings attributed to Jesus.

[6] Pistis Sophia dated 3rd to 4th century AD. Teachings of Transfigured Jesus to his disciples.

among women", and "Blessed are you who believed that what was spoken to you by the Lord would be fulfilled", in the canonical Gospel of Luke.

The vision of the Jerusalem Christians as the continuing Temple is perhaps important for our understanding of Mary Magdalene. Margaret Barker has shown that in First Temple Theology the earthly mother of the King/High Priest is very significant. She is the mirror image of her heavenly counterpart. She is portrayed as the Lady in the Temple. If Magdalene is a rough transliteration of the Woman in the Tower where tower is an image for the Holy of Holies c.f. the watch-tower in the vineyard (Isaiah 5:2), we have a pointer to a Temple figure who would fit the early Hebrew Christians seeing themselves as the true Temple. I think that we are given enough evidence that Jesus, John the Baptist and others were looking for a restoration of the first Temple, the true Temple. Even Jesus' friend Lazarus could be from a First Temple High Priestly family. Lazarus was the shortened familiar form of Eleazar.

In this traditional scheme Mary, his mother, could qualify as the Lady in the Tower and as exalted. She is the mother of the King of the Jews and the High Priest who performed the Atonement sacrifice. I now ask my big question. Could Magdalene be a post-crucifixion, post-resurrection title given to Mary of Nazareth by the earliest Jerusalem Christians for whom she was the mother of their High Priest and their King and used retrospectively by the Gospel writers? This would suit the Pillars and John who looks after her, and takes her from Jerusalem in the Jewish War in one of those periods of Roman generosity to be with him in Asia Minor. Eusebius, a bishop in Palestine in the early 4th century, tells us how people heeded the oracle in Revelation 18:4-5 and fled east towards Pella. (*History* 5.13) For Paul she would be yet another example of all he was fighting against. This is a battle Paul is doomed to lose in Ephesus so that he is no longer able to go there. This has to be a balanced judgment. Acts 20:16f is only convincing as an itinerary. That Paul is in a hurry does not fit well with the stop at Miletus to meet the Ephesian delegates and a set piece Lukan speech that will inevitably cause delay. 2 Corinthians 1:8f tells what a tough time Paul had at Ephesus and is a good indicator of why he would not return there on his journey to Jerusalem. His whole mission there is under attack. That just leaves the question of how you interpret Romans 15:23. Is it job done, no more work to do, or is it any future work is now prevented? We may ask ourselves when it is that Peter goes to Rome. Does he go with Paul?

We can now introduce into our journey Mary of Nazareth as a major interest. It was with some general questions that I began my journey in my garden. Who was most likely to be at Jesus' death? Whom would he have loved more than anyone else? Who would be anxious to visit his tomb? Who would want to clasp hold of him and not let go? I gave the tentative answer, his mother. Can this one be worked out?

Jesus' mother is never named by John and elsewhere appears only in the birth narratives and Acts 1:14 by name. Except for once in John 19:25 she never appears along with Mary Magdalene. John 19:25-27 are difficult and read rather awkwardly. Leaving aside whether these verses are plausible or not (Barrett op.cit.supra p.458), whether there was a redactor/editor or not, whether the text is displaced or just confused, we need to see what the text as it stands, left like this by the final hand, might reasonably have to say to us. First, it says Jesus entrusted his mother to the beloved disciple. This is a genuine personal gesture. But it is also an explanation for how the beloved disciple, John, has care of Jesus' mother, which tradition says he did have. This is the tradition of the Johannine Church. If others wish to say this is a role that John has taken upon himself with no authority, this can now be denied by the words of Jesus himself. Personal rivalry is always at play in the Church.

Secondly, there is the word of address that Jesus uses to his mother, *gunai*. In his commentary on John, Professor Grayston (Kenneth Grayston *Gospel of John*, 1990) notes the similarity of address by Jesus to his mother in 19:26 with his address to her at Cana 2:4 (pp.30-31;162). "Once more Jesus addresses his mother with grave courtesy as he did at Cana. 'Woman', *gunai* in Greek, is an address of formal courtesy (almost 'my lady'). It is common enough in ordinary speech but most surprising from a son addressing his mother. From that previous episode we know that she is a mother in Israel (i.e. she leads the Jewish component of the future Christian community, she can detect a Yes within a daunting No, and she tells people to obey Jesus). It is not by chance that in doing the will of his Father he is prompted by his mother; nor is it by chance that the Jewish component of the later community is validated by a mother in Israel who says, 'Do whatever he tells you'." This would point to a person of status, influence and vision, someone who would be qualified to be Magdalene, exalted. Jesus is here pointing to his mother in her role as the Great Lady of the Temple. He does the same thing again in 19:25. When it comes to the listing of the women at the cross the writer refers to her also by her earthly title of Mary Magdalene.

Intriguingly, when the angels and the risen Jesus address Mary Magdalene in the garden in John 20 they address her as 'woman', 'my lady' exactly the same Greek word that is used at Cana and at the crucifixion by Jesus to his mother. Is this John's final pointer to her identity?

Ephrem the Syrian (d 373AD) was a biblical scholar and hymn writer. In his commentary on the fourfold Gospel, the Diatesseron, he said four times that the Mary who met Jesus at the tomb was his mother, not Mary Magdalene, and in one of his hymns he wrote:

> It is clear that Virginity is greater and nobler than Holiness
> For it is She who bore the Son and gave Him milk from her breast;
> It was She who sat at his feet and did Him service by washing.
> At the cross She was beside Him and in the resurrection She saw Him.
> (R. Murray *Symbols of Church and Kingdom,* 1975, p.330)

If Ephrem is correct we have here an identification of the woman who washed Jesus feet in Mark and Luke- one that did not try to malign her. Did the Syrian Church know another version of that story?

The earliest Gospel book, using the Syriac text, was made in the late 6th Century by a scribe named Rabbula. He showed Mary of Nazareth at the crucifixion, and then twice at the tomb: hearing the angel and falling at the feet of Jesus. He also showed Mary of Nazareth at the Ascension and at Pentecost. It is quite clear that he intended the same person in all five scenes. Both here and in Ephrem this is in line with the Old Syriac text of John 20:1 and 18 (vid.supra.)

At risk of over-speculation, it might be that the writer of Acts knew about Mary's presence at the Ascension and at Pentecost as she is named as being in the immediate post-Ascension group of believers (Acts 1:14)

In the Babylonian Talmud *Shabbat 104b,* a compendium of Jewish law and lore compiled about 500AD, Miriam, the mother of Jesus, was a woman weaver of hair (megaddela neshayia), clearly wordplay on Magdalene as both share the same root (Barker *King of the Jews,* 2014, p.576). Remember this is Jews now talking about Jesus' mother. This is how they knew her, as Magdalene. They could have misunderstood her name or they could have been ridiculing the Christians. "You call her exalted, the tower, but she is really just a hairdresser."

Jesus mother comes in for lots of insults even in Jesus' own lifetime. In the same passage in the Talmud she was known as Stada, which means 'she who has turned aside from her husband'. So Jesus was Ben Stada, the son of an unfaithful woman. In *Shabbat* 106a 'she played the harlot with carpenters'. Is she a prostitute? 'Hairdresser' is an euphemism for prostitute. Is this the origin of Mary Magdalene the prostitute?

Dan Jaffe *(The Virgin Birth of Jesus in the Talmudic Context -a Philological and Historical Analysis. Laval theologique et philosophique volume 68. 3, 2012)* examines in some detail in an historical and philological study the material relating to another title for Jesus, ben Pantera. Pantera was a fairly common name in the Roman army. Jesus was the son of a Roman soldier. He concludes: 'that this ancient expression has to be understood as corresponding to a period in which the Jews wished to think of Christianity, choosing the person of Jesus as an emblematic figure of this reality. The expression ben Pantera expresses mockery of and even scorn towards Jesus. It must be placed back in a period in which, on account of the doctrinal controversies between Jews and Christians, the two religions had consummated a Parting of the Ways and acknowledged each other as rivals. Thus ben Pantera appears to be the oldest mention of Jesus in the Talmuduc literature'.

'It is suggested that we see in the name ben Pantera a mockery of the Christian belief in the conception and virginal birth of Jesus. The accusation of an illegitimate union set out and conveyed into the Jewish world as well as into the pagan world is found in Talmudic, principally Tannaitic, literature. Christianity is often likened there to the seduction exercised by prostitution'.

John's Gospel itself gives us a hint that something similar was being said about Jesus, perhaps in his own lifetime or at least in the period of the

Gospel. John 8:41 says: 'They said to him, "We were not born of fornication, we have one Father, even God."' The separate pronoun, 'we', gives strength to the statement. 'Unlike you, we were not born of fornication.'

There was also the accusation of Celsus.

'After this he represents the Jew as having a conversation with Jesus himself and refuting him on many charges, as he thinks: first, because "he fabricated the story of his birth from a virgin; and he reproaches him because he came from a Jewish village and from a poor country woman who earned her living by spinning". He says that "she was driven out by her husband, who was a carpenter by trade, as she was convicted of adultery". Then he says that "after she had been driven out by her husband and while she was wandering about in a disgraceful way she secretly gave birth to Jesus".

Let us return, however, to the words put into the mouth of the Jew, where "the mother of Jesus" is described as having been "turned out by the carpenter who was betrothed to her, as she had been convicted of adultery and had a child by a certain soldier named Panthera"'.
(Chadwick *Origen "Contra Celsum"* I. 28,32)

Intriguingly at the same period as the Babylonian Talmud was taking shape (compiled about 500AD, though it continued to be edited later) Byzantine hymnody was also developing using long established themes. The Akathist Hymn to Mary Theotokos existed for the most part before it was officially accepted by the Church in 626AD. In this hymn, stanza 23, Mary is described as 'unshakeable Tower of the Church, impregnable fortress of the Kingdom'.

Three hundred years later, in the 9th century, the Small Paraklesis (Intercessory Prayer) to the Most Holy Theotokos was composed. It concludes with these words: You are a tower adorned with gold, a city surrounded by 12 walls, a strong throne touched by the sun, a royal seat for the king, O unexplainable wonder, how do you nurse the Master?

While one cannot suggest there was any direct connection between the writers of the Babylonian Talmud and the Akathist Hymn, one can reasonably say they both developed in the same milieu and so would be familiar with prevailing ideas.

The last two pieces of tangential evidence are two buildings. Buildings sadly are as fragile as papyrus especially in areas prone to earthquake and strife.

The first is the huge church built in Jerusalem, 400 years after Jerusalem had been destroyed, and funded by the Emperor Justinian. It was the New Church of the Theotokos, known as the Nea. It was intended to be the new Temple of Solomon, but it was destroyed in war in 614AD. It is not built according to Revelation's heavenly measurements but rather the measurements of the restored Temple revealed to Ezekiel. These are almost exactly the measurements of the Nea as discovered by archaeologists. The Nea was to be the Temple restored as a tower. To this the Great Lady would return. But this is the Christian Temple and it is dedicated to the Theotokos, Mary of Nazareth. She is the Great Lady, mgdlh.

The other building is Hagia Sophia in Constantinople, again the work of the Emperor Justinian. The present building is the third on the site dedicated to Hagia Sophia, Holy Wisdom, one of the names of the Great Lady in the Temple. Who she was believed to be is clearly revealed by the great image of Mary, the Theotokos, and her Son. Mary is Hagia Sophia. Sadly, history has once again driven her from her temple as this great church was converted into a mosque in 1453, then made a Museum in 1935, and has now become a mosque again. Taken from the Christians, there seems no mind to return it to the Church.

As we approach the end of our journey we need to return to John 20.

Here we have seen Mary Magdalene as witness of the Ascension and by implication present at the giving of the Spirit in the upper room, Pentecost. This would seem to tie Mary Magdalene/Mary of Nazareth in with the Ascension and Pentecost as shown by Rabbula (vid supra).

For the moment we have reached the end of our journey. I believe I have found that Mary of Nazareth is Mary Magdalene. The subject of the Gospel of Mary is one and the same person, Mary of Nazareth alias Mary Magdalene. Wherever we see Mary Magdalene we see also Mary of Nazareth.